Amazing
AMERICAN CURLS

GENTLE! UNIQUE! LOVING!

ELEGANT! CURIOUS! ALERT!

ABDO
Publishing Company

Katherine Hengel

Consulting Editor, Diane Craig, M.A./Reading Specialist

visit us at www.abdopublishing.com

Published by ABDO Publishing Company, a division of ABDO, P.O. Box 398166, Minneapolis, Minnesota 55439. Copyright © 2012 by Abdo Consulting Group, Inc. International copyrights reserved in all countries. No part of this book may be reproduced in any form without written permission from the publisher. Super SandCastle™ is a trademark and logo of ABDO Publishing Company.

Printed in the United States of America, North Mankato, Minnesota
062011
092011

 PRINTED ON RECYCLED PAPER

Editor: Liz Salzmann
Content Developer: Nancy Tuminelly
Cover and Interior Design and Production:
   Anders Hanson, Mighty Media
Illustrations: Bob Doucet
Photo Credits: Shutterstock

Library of Congress Cataloging-in-Publication Data
Hengel, Katherine.
  Amazing American curls / authored by Katherine Hengel ; illustrated by Bob Doucet.
    p. cm. -- (Cat craze. set 2)
  ISBN 978-1-61714-829-3
  1. American curl cat--Juvenile literature. I. Doucet, Bob, ill. II. Title. III. Series.

  SF449.A44H46 2012
  636.8--dc22

                    2010053007

Super SandCastle™ books are created by a team of professional educators, reading specialists, and content developers around five essential components—phonemic awareness, phonics, vocabulary, text comprehension, and fluency—to assist young readers as they develop reading skills and strategies and increase their general knowledge. All books are written, reviewed, and leveled for guided reading, early reading intervention, and Accelerated Reader® programs for use in shared, guided, and independent reading and writing activities to support a balanced approach to literacy instruction.

CONTENTS

The
AMERICAN CURL

American curls are loving cats with ears that curl back. They have beautiful, **silky** coats. American curls act like curious kittens for their whole lives! They are nicknamed the Peter Pans of cats.

FACIAL FEATURES

Head

An American curl's head has a rounded wedge shape. It is a little longer than it is wide.

Muzzle

The American curl has a straight, medium-sized **muzzle**.

Eyes

American curls have large, walnut-shaped eyes.

Ears

Their ears curl backward and have round tips. They can curl a little bit or a lot!

4

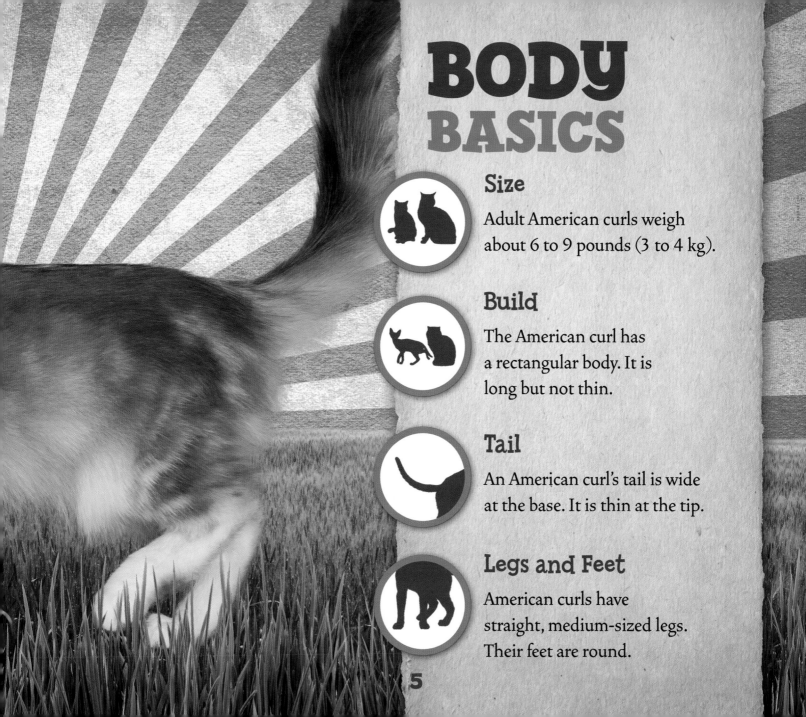

BODY
BASICS

Size

Adult American curls weigh about 6 to 9 pounds (3 to 4 kg).

Build

The American curl has a rectangular body. It is long but not thin.

Tail

An American curl's tail is wide at the base. It is thin at the tip.

Legs and Feet

American curls have straight, medium-sized legs. Their feet are round.

COAT & COLOR

American Curl Fur

American curls can have long or short hair. Their coats can be just about any color or pattern!

Longhair American curls have fine, **silky** coats. The coat hangs smooth and flat. They also have full, fluffy tails! Shorthair American curls have soft, flat coats. Both kinds shed very little. Their coats don't need much **grooming**!

ORANGE FUR

LONGHAIR CALICO

American curls come in many different colors and patterns.
The photos on these pages show just a few examples.

BLACK FUR

FAWN FUR

BROWN FUR

LONGHAIR TABBY

SHORTHAIR SOLID BLACK

SHORTHAIR SOLID WHITE

HEALTH & CARE

Life Span

American curls can live for 15 years or longer!

Health Concerns

American curls are very healthy cats! They do not need much **grooming**. But their ears may need special cleaning sometimes.

VET'S CHECKLIST

- Have your American curl spayed or neutered. This will prevent unwanted kittens.

- Visit a vet for regular checkups.

- Ask your vet which types of food and litter are right for your American curl.

- Clean your American curl's teeth and ears once a week.

- Ask your vet about shots that may benefit your cat.

ATTITUDE & BEHAVIOR

Personality

American curls are curious and intelligent. They love to be around people and other animals. They are very **social** and loving. They follow their owners around all day long! They don't meow very much. They coo instead!

Activity Level

American curls have a lot of energy. They want to be involved in everything their owners are doing! They'll even try to get in the shower with you! American curls love challenges and adventures. They can even be taught to play fetch!

All About Me

Hi! My name is Arthur. I'm an American curl. I just wanted to let you know a few things about me. I made some lists below of things I like and dislike.

Things I Like

- Sitting on my owner's lap
- Playing with other animals
- Learning new things
- Being included in my owner's activities
- Playing with toys
- Cuddling with people
- Helping my owner do things

Things I Dislike

- Being alone
- Getting bored
- Not having anyone to follow around
- Lack of activity in my home

LITTERS & KITTENS

Litter Size

Female American curls usually give birth to three to five kittens.

Diet

Newborn kittens drink their mother's milk. They can begin to eat kitten food when they are about six weeks old. Kitten food is different from cat food. It has the extra **protein**, fat, **vitamins**, and **minerals** that kittens need to grow.

Growth

American curl kittens should stay with their mothers until they are two to three months old. An American curl will be full grown when it is about one year old.

When American curls are born, their ears are straight. They start to curl within 10 days. After about four months they stop changing.

BUYING AN AMERICAN CURL

Choosing a Breeder

It's best to buy a kitten from a **breeder**, not a pet store. When you visit a cat breeder, ask to see the mother and father of the kittens. Make sure the parents are healthy, friendly, and well behaved.

Picking a Kitten

Choose a kitten that isn't too active or too shy. If you sit down, some of the kittens may come over to you. One of them might be the right one for you!

Is It the Right Cat for You?

Buying a cat is a big decision. You'll want to make sure your new pet suits your lifestyle.

Get out a piece of paper. Draw a line down the middle.

Read the statements listed here. Each time you agree with a statement from the left column, make a mark on the left side of your paper. When you agree with a statement from the right column, make a mark on the right side of your paper.

I want to spend a lot of time with my cat.	☐ ☐	I don't want a cat that needs a lot of attention.
My cat should be good around children.	☐ ☐	It doesn't matter if my cat is good around kids.
My cat should like being around other animals.	☐ ☐	My cat will never be around other animals.
I don't want to **groom** my cat very often.	☐ ☐	I really like grooming cats.
I want a cat that doesn't shed too much.	☐ ☐	I don't mind cleaning up cat hair.

If you made more marks on the left side than on the right side, an American curl may be the right cat for you! If you made more marks on the right side of your paper, you might want to consider another breed.

Some Things You'll Need

Cats go to the bathroom in a **litter box**. It should be kept in a quiet place. Most cats learn to use their litter box all by themselves. You just have to show them where it is! The dirty **litter** should be scooped out every day. The litter should be changed completely every week.

Your cat's **food and water dishes** should be wide and shallow. This helps your cat keep its whiskers clean. The dishes should be in a different area than the litter box. Cats do not like to eat and go to the bathroom in the same area.

Cats love to scratch! **Scratching posts** help keep cats from scratching the furniture. The scratching post should be taller than your cat. It should have a wide, heavy base so it won't tip over.

Cats are natural predators. Without small animals to hunt, cats may become bored and unhappy. **Cat toys** can satisfy your cat's need to chase and capture. They will help keep your cat entertained and happy.

Cats should not play with balls of yarn or string. If they accidentally eat the yarn, they could get sick.

Cat claws should be trimmed regularly with special cat claw **clippers**. Regular nail clippers will also work. Some people choose to have their cat's claws removed by a vet. But most vets and animal rights groups think declawing is cruel.

You should brush your cat regularly with a **cat hair brush**. This will help keep its coat healthy and clean.

A **cat bed** will give your cat a safe, comfortable place to sleep.

LIVING WITH AN AMERICAN CURL

Being a Good Companion

American curls are very **social**. They want to be with their owners all the time. They love to sit with people and be petted. It's important to give them a lot of attention.

Inside or Outside?

It's a good idea to keep your American curl inside. Most vets and **breeders** agree that it is best for cats to be kept inside. That way the cats are safe from predators and cars.

Feeding Your American Curl

American curls may be fed regular cat food. Your vet can help you choose the best food for your cat.

Cleaning the Litter Box

Like all cats, American curls like to be clean. They don't like smelly or dirty litter boxes. If the litter box is dirty, they may go to the bathroom somewhere else. Ask your vet for advice if your cat isn't using its box.

☠ # DANGER: POISONOUS FOODS

Some people like to feed their cats table scraps. Here are some human foods that can make cats sick.

TOMATOES

POTATOES

ONIONS

GARLIC

CHOCOLATE

GRAPES

19

THE STRAY THAT STARTED IT ALL

Some cat **breeds** have been around for centuries. But the American curl is pretty new! It was discovered in 1981. On a hot June day, Joe and Grace Ruga found a **stray** cat at their door. The cat had funny ears and long, black hair.

Joe and Grace took her in and named her Shulamith. She is the original American curl! She had four kittens in her first litter. Two of them had curled ears! Shulamith had started a new **breed** and a worldwide **sensation**!

FIND THE
AMERICAN CURL

A

B

C

D

THE AMERICAN CURL QUIZ

1. American curls are nicknamed the Peter Pans of cats. **True or false?**

2. American curls have very small eyes. **True or false?**

3. American curls always have long hair. **True or false?**

4. American curls are very healthy cats. **True or false?**

5. American curls love to be around people. **True or false?**

6. American curl kittens are born with curled ears. **True or false?**

Answers: **1)** true **2)** false **3)** false **4)** true **5)** true **6)** false

GLOSSARY

breed - a group of animals or plants with common ancestors. A *breeder* is someone whose job is to breed certain animals or plants.

groom - to clean the fur of an animal.

mineral - a natural element that plants, animals, and people need to be healthy.

muzzle - the nose and jaws of an animal.

protein - a substance found in all plant and animal cells.

sensation - a cause of a lot of excitement.

silky - being soft and smooth, like silk.

social - enjoying the company of others.

stray - 1. a pet that is wandering around or lost. 2. having wandered away or gotten lost.

vitamin - a substance needed for good health, found naturally in plants and meats.